Even the Sound Waves Obey Him

Bible Stories Brought to Life with Science

Nancy B. Kennedy • Illustrated by Dana Regan

CONCORDIA PUBLISHING HOUSE • SAINT LOUIS

Published by Concordia Publishing House

3558 S. Jefferson Avenue

St. Louis, MO 63118-3968

1-800-325-3040   www.cph.org

Illustrated by Dana Regan

Manufactured in the United States of America

1	2	3	4	5	6	7	8	9	10
14	13	12	11	10	09	08	07	06	05

For John and Evan,
who are in this
great experiment with me

-NBK

Contents

Part 2: New Testament Stories

Note to the Reader

It seems silly now, but when I first started thinking about parenthood, one of the things I feared most was The Art Project. While many people can wield scissors, paint, crayons, and glue with some measure of mastery, I cannot. The thought of spending hours with a child hunched over stacks of supplies struggling to make a credible ark unnerved me.

But the Lord knows us through and through. Graciously, He gave my husband and me a child who has little to no interest in making things. When he glues, he wants his hands washed off immediately. He will color, but only when forced. Mess with paint? Not him.

This blessing presents a problem, though, when it comes to family devotions. When Evan was an infant, John and I used music to reinforce Bible stories, marching around the living room with instruments, singing Sunday school songs. Sometime before Evan's third birthday, we began with a children's Bible that suggested hand motions and posed simple questions. He was happy enough with that for a few days. Then he began to protest "the Jesus book." We moved on to lift-the-flap books and even one with removable blocks that are rearranged to tell a story. Each kept him occupied for a few days. Then the whining would begin again.

I mulled this over for a while. I looked at Sunday School activity books and found mountains of material for people who relish the challenge of transforming toilet paper rolls, cotton balls, toothpicks and coffee cans into Bible story props. I found nature-themed material that encouraged children to learn Bible lessons from the world around them. Again, not for us. When Evan takes a walk, he's a man on a mission. He wants to get to the park or his friend's house, and he's not going to stop for leaves, stones, or small animals. Projects that involve edibles—like the Tower of Babel made with graham crackers and candy corn—are out too. To his way of thinking, food (especially candy) is to be consumed, not played with.

Then one day at my sister's house, my brother-in-law took the kids into the kitchen and showed them how to make an icky mud using just cornstarch and water. An idea began to take shape. Would Evan be interested in Bible stories if they were accompanied by simple, scientific activities that allowed him to participate in a way he enjoyed? I already knew he liked to help in the kitchen, cracking eggs, mixing pancake batter, and scooping out cookie dough.

We tried a few activities—scattering pepper across the surface of water, making oil blobs dance in a glass of water. Evan loved it. One morning, when he said he wanted to make the oil blobs again, I was jubilant. This could be the very thing. I spent many hours with many sources researching simple activities we could do together. When I had collected a folder full of notes and ideas, the concept for this book solidified.

In this collection, you'll find forty-four familiar Bible stories paired with simple, scientific activities that you and your child—or a teacher and students—can read and then do together. When deciding which activities to include, I kept the following in mind:

The activities had to be safe enough for preschoolers. I omitted any activities using matches, boiling water or rubbing alcohol, no matter how tempting they were. Even when you're right there with your child, you know how quickly something can happen.

The ingredients had to be easily found around the house or classroom. One intriguing experiment I saw called for beet juice. Beet juice? Sorry, but my pantry's not that well stocked. I did relent once or twice when I thought the activities were too fun to ignore and the items could easily be found in a pharmacy or grocery store.

The activities had to work, and work fast. I did make a few exceptions—what's a rule without them? But all of the activities produce reliable results, and all but one or two immediately because you know the attention span of a preschooler.

The instructions couldn't be too complex (because you know the attention span of an adult).

The science explanations had to be easy. If I can understand it, anyone can. Trust me.

I hope you enjoy these activities as much as we do. If you find this is your child's bent, look at the book titles and websites listed at the end of the book. They contain plenty of projects to please your child now and some that will become more appropriate as he or she gets older. I know I'll be consulting science books for years to come. My son is now in first grade and his least favorite class is—you guessed it—art.

Nancy Kennedy, Spring 2005

Note: *The activities in this book are complete on one page. Each includes a short and simple review of the Bible story intended to be read (or told) to the child. In addition to that, a section called "What We Can Learn" is offered to give the adult some background information about the Bible story and its Gospel connection. The activities themselves are introduced with a short purpose statement, a list of materials needed, step-by-step directions, and an easy-to-understand, straightforward explanation of the science underlying the activity.*

Part 1:

Old Testament Stories

Before You and Me

Genesis 1-2

In the beginning, before there was anything, God was there.

When the time was right, He made everything from nothing. It was a miracle called creation. He made the heavens and the earth, the day and the night, the sun and the moon and stars. He made birds for the air and fish for the sea. He made wild animals and tame animals, snakes that slither, and creatures that crawl.

And then, when everything was just right, God made Adam and Eve from the dust of the earth. He breathed His own life into them. He made them in His image and they were holy. And He loved them most of all.

When He was done He said, "It is good."

What We Can Learn

God created each of us to be unique, but we all have one thing in common—our sinfulness. When Adam and Eve fell into sinfulness, our heavenly Father promised to make things right again. He did this by sending His Son, Jesus, to pay the penalty of our sins by giving His life on the cross. Those who believe in Jesus as their Savior and repent of their sins have forgiveness and the promise of eternal life in heaven.

What You Need

Spoons

Spoon Faces

God created us in His image. Let's look at ourselves using a spoon instead of a mirror.

What You Do

- *Pick up a spoon by the handle with the bowl up and facing away from you. (Spoons with a shiny finish work best.) What do you see?*

- *Now turn the spoon around with the inside of the bowl facing you. What do you see now?*

What's Happening

The spoon gives back your reflection, just as a mirror would. The mirror's shape—convex when you look at the back of the spoon and concave when you look at the front—distorts your image. A convex mirror creates an image that is smaller and right side up, while a concave mirror creates an image that is upside down.

Swinging Cereal

Because of their sin, Adam and Eve were driven from the Garden of Eden. Let's see how we can attract and then drive away an object using static electricity.

What You Do

- *Snip off a foot-long piece of thread and tie one end around a cereal O. Tape the other end to a surface, such as a tabletop, that leaves the thread swinging freely.*

- *Inflate the balloon and tie it. Rub it vigorously against a wool sweater, coat, or scarf. (If you use a comb instead, run it through your hair several times.)*

- *Bring the balloon (or comb) a few inches from the cereal and watch what happens.*

What's Happening

When you rub a balloon, it becomes charged with electrons, giving it a negative charge. The cereal, initially having a neutral charge, becomes positively charged when its negatively charged electrons move away from the balloon. It is then attracted to the balloon and swings over. Once they touch, electrons slowly move from the balloon to the cereal, giving both a negative charge. The cereal drops away and then jumps away from the balloon if you try to bring it near.

Adam and Eve Disobey God

Genesis 3

Adam and Eve didn't live in their garden for long. Although it made Him sad, God had to make them leave.

To live in peace with God, He told them to obey one rule. They could not eat the fruit from one tree. But one day Satan, disguised as a snake, tempted Eve to eat that fruit. She did. Adam took a bite, too, although he knew it was wrong.

When they broke God's law, they knew they had sinned. Their sin made God angry, and He sent them away from the garden. He promised that one day His Son, Jesus, would bring us back to God.

What We Can Learn

Sin came into the world through one man—Adam. In the same way forgiveness came into the world through one man—Jesus. Jesus lived a perfect life in our place, He took the punishment for sin in our place, and He conquered death in our place. Because of Jesus, we have forgiveness and the hope of eternal life. Because of Jesus, we will live forever in heaven.

God Starts Over

Genesis 6–9

It made God very sad and angry to see people give in to all the evil in their hearts. Wouldn't it be better if He had never made them?

But Noah and his family were faithful to God. So God said to Noah, "Make an ark."

Noah did, and his family and pairs of all the animals walked up into the ark. God shut the door behind them. He sent a flood, a great gushing of water from the earth and rain from the sky to wash the world clean.

When it was safe, God dried up the land, and Noah and his family and all the animals stepped out onto dry ground. They saw in the sky a beautiful rainbow—God's promise never again to destroy His creation by flood.

What We Can Learn

This Bible story shows us two things—God's judgment on sin and the salvation He offers His faithful people. In the Flood, God washed the world of those who were not sorry for their sins, those who rebelled against God. Yet He kept His promise to bring faithful Noah and his family safely through the water—just as we are saved through the waters of Holy Baptism. God washes us of our sin through the death and resurrection of Jesus Christ. Through water and Word, God keeps His promise to save us from sin and deliver us from eternal death.

Miniature Rainbow

God used a rainbow to promise that He would never again flood the earth. Let's make an indoor rainbow of our own.

What You Need

Tall, clear glass
Water
Sunny window
White paper

What You Do

- *Fill the glass to the rim with water. (Other clear containers like pitchers work too.)*

- *Place the glass on the sill of a sunny window.*

- *Position the paper on the floor (or the wall) to catch the rainbow. What does it look like?*

What's Happening

Light is not colorless—it is actually made up of seven colors. In what is called the visible light spectrum, each color vibrates at a different speed. When sunlight passes through the water, the colors are slowed down and bent individually to produce the seven color bands of the rainbow.

Building a Tall Tower

Genesis 11:1–9

Have you ever built a sand castle? You know how much fun that can be.

Long ago, when everyone in the world spoke the same language, all the people of one town called Babel said, "Let's build a tower that touches heaven." They were proud of themselves. They wanted to show how great they were.

They made mud bricks and began to build. Up and up, higher and higher. It was a tall, tall tower. But the Lord saw what they were doing. He knew what they were thinking. He put strange words into their mouths so no one knew what another one said. They were confused. The building stopped, and the people scattered.

Chattering Coin

God scattered people across the earth and made them speak different languages. Let's make a coin "talk" to us in its own language.

What You Need

- **Cup**
- **Water**
- **Large coin**
- **Soda bottle**
- **Freezer**

What We Can Learn

When the people of Babel chose to make a name for themselves, they chose to put themselves above God. He scattered them and confused their language, showing that no one can rebel against Him and endure. God brings believers together, though, in one place—the church. There we receive forgiveness by hearing His Word and receiving the Sacraments, There He unites us and comes to us with His grace and mercy.

What You Do

- *Fill the cup with water and drop in the coin. (Something larger than a quarter works best—try 50–cent pieces, souvenir coins, or foreign coins such as the British pence.)*

- *Put the uncapped empty soda bottle in the freezer for five to ten minutes.*

- *Take out the bottle and put it on a flat surface like a sink or countertop. Cover the mouth of the bottle with the wet coin. What happens?*

What's Happening

Cold air contracts, which means it takes up less space. When you put a bottle in the freezer, the air molecules inside cool and move closer together. When you take it out, the air molecules inside warm up and expand but are trapped by the coin. (The water on the coin creates a seal.) The air pushes upward and builds up enough pressure to lift the coin, making it rattle.

Visitors from Heaven

Genesis 18:1-15

Abraham was old—almost 100 years old—and so was his wife, Sarah. One day when he was outside his tent, Abraham saw three visitors approaching. "Please sit and rest," he invited them. Abraham and Sarah cooked for them a meal of meat, bread, butter, and milk.

These visitors were angels from heaven. The angel of the Lord told the couple they would have a son. Through this boy, God would bless Abraham and his family. He would make them a great nation and raise up our Savior.

But Abraham and Sarah were too old to have children and Sarah laughed at what the visitors said. People their age didn't have babies!

Then, a year later, Sarah gave birth to Isaac. Is anything too hard for the Lord?

What We Can Learn

When the Lord told Abraham and Sarah they would have a son, Sarah laughed out loud. After all, she was nearly 100 also and childless. Yet it happened just as God said it would. Through this elderly couple, the Lord God ensured a lineage for Jesus and prepared the way for His plan to bring forgiveness and salvation to His people. Indeed, nothing is too hard for the Lord!

Shaker Butter

Abraham and Sarah prepared a hearty meal for their heavenly visitors, including homemade bread and butter. It's easy to make butter yourself.

What You Need

Heavy cream
Baby food jar
Measuring spoon
Crackers or bread
Butter knife

What You Do

- *Put 1 tablespoon of heavy cream into the jar.*

- *Shake the jar vigorously for several minutes. (Pass it to the next person when your arm gets tired!) What happens?*

What's Happening

The cream is a mixture of fat droplets dispersed in water. Shaking the jar causes the fat droplets to clump together, forcing out the water (or buttermilk), which is the excess liquid in the jar. Spread the butter on your crackers and enjoy!

Jacob's Dream

Genesis 28:10-20

Abraham had a grandson whose name was Jacob. Jacob was traveling a long way when he stopped for the night in a rocky field. He was tired from his journey, so, using a stone as a pillow, he lay down to sleep.

What a dream he had! He saw a great stairway stretching up to heaven, and angels walking up and down. Above it all stood the Lord, the God of Abraham, who said, "I am with you."

When he awoke, Jacob knew he had seen God. "Surely, the Lord is in this place!"

What We Can Learn

As Jacob slept, God opened heaven to him. Jacob, in turn, marked the spot to memorialize it, remembering that God would be with him always. Jacob felt this place was special—the house of God and the gate to heaven—so he named the place Bethel, which means "the house of God." For us, Jesus is the gate to heaven. In His death on the cross and resurrection from the grave, Jesus opened heaven to us. His sacrifice brings us forgiveness of sins. This is how Christians participate in the blessings of heaven as Jacob did.

Rising Sun

Jacob dreamed of a stairway stretching from heaven to earth. Let's make the "sun" rise on Jacob after his dream.

What You Need

Measuring cup
Rapid-rise yeast
Warm water
Corn syrup
Small water or soda bottle
Funnel
Balloon
Masking tape

What You Do

- *In a measuring cup, dissolve a packet of dry yeast in 1/4 cup of warm water. Stir to mix.*

- *Mix 1/2 cup of corn syrup into the cup. (You can also use 2 tablespoons of sugar. Make sure it dissolves.)*

- *Pour the solution into a small clean bottle, such as a water bottle, using a funnel.*

- *Fit an uninflated balloon over the opening of the bottle and seal it well with masking tape.*

- *Shake the bottle and set it on a countertop or windowsill. Watch the bottle over the next few hours. What happens?*

What's Happening

When combined, yeast (a fungus) and sugar ferment and release carbon dioxide and alcohol—that's the foamy top that forms inside the bottle. The carbon dioxide gas inflates the balloon over time.

Joseph's Colorful Coat

Genesis 37-41

Jacob had not one, not two, but twelve sons. He loved Joseph more than the others. To him Jacob gave a colorful coat, one more beautiful than the other boys had. Joseph's brothers were angry because Joseph was Jacob's favorite son.

One day while they were far from home, the brothers threw Joseph into a deep well. They were going to leave him there, but along came some traders. The brothers brought Joseph up from the pit and sold him as a slave to the traders.

But God was watching over Joseph, making sure he was safe. When Joseph was grown, he became a great ruler and his brothers bowed down to him.

What We Can Learn

This well-known Bible story is a perfect example of God's special plans for His children. God chose Joseph to lead and provide for his people. God placed Joseph in the right place at the right time to carry out His plan. Also in His time and according to His plan, God provided His Son—Jesus—to die for our sin. In His own time, God again carried out His plan through Jesus' birth in Bethlehem so He could pay for our sins on the cross.

Color Wheel

Jacob gave his son Joseph a beautiful coat decorated with all the colors of the rainbow. We can make the many colors of the coat look like just one color.

What You Need

White cardboard or heavy paper
Cup or bowl
Scissors
Pencil
Ruler
Crayons

What You Do

*   *Using a cup or bowl, trace a circle on the cardboard or paper.*
*   *Divide the circle into six equal wedges, using the ruler.*
*   *Color the six sections clockwise with the following colors: blue, violet, red, orange, yellow, green.*
*   *Poke a hole through the middle of the wheel and put the pencil through the hole.*
*   *Hold the pencil horizontally and spin the wheel as fast as you can. What do you see?*

What's Happening

The colors of the wheel are the colors that combine to create white light. When you spin the wheel fast enough, the colors blend together and appear as just one color—white.

Baby Moses Rescued

Exodus 2:1-10

Joseph's family came to live in Egypt. In time his family—the Israelites—became so big that the Egyptians were afraid of them. They made the Israelites their slaves.

Pharaoh, the Egyptian king, wanted to kill the slaves' baby boys. But one mother put her baby into a basket and floated him in the River Nile.

Along came Pharaoh's daughter, who heard the baby crying. She plucked him from the river and raised baby Moses as her own. She even chose his own mother to care for him.

God protected Moses so one day he could free His people from slavery.

What We Can Learn

The story of baby Moses continues a theme we often see in the Old Testament—a death sentence and an escape to life. It also mirrors a theme in our own lives—our sin dooms us to eternal death, but through His death in our place, our Savior provides us with a means of escape from the slavery of sin—forgiveness. In Baptism, we die with Christ and rise to new life.

Ice Rescue

One of Pharaoh's daughters rescued the baby Moses from the Nile River. Let's see how we can rescue an ice cube from a glass of water.

What You Need

Water
Drinking glass
Ice cube
Embroidery thread or string
Salt

What You Do

- *Fill the glass with water and drop in an ice cube.*
- *Lay the thread or string across the top of the ice cube.*
- *Sprinkle the ice cube with salt and wait a few seconds.*
- *Try to lift the ice cube using the thread. Can you?*

What's Happening

When you pour salt on an ice cube, it dissolves into the water of the ice. Saltwater freezes at a lower temperature than the temperature at which freshwater freezes, so the ice melts. But the coldness of the ice cube refreezes the water, putting a layer of ice over the thread and trapping it. You can lift the ice cube right out of the water!

The Plagues of Egypt

Exodus 5-11

The Israelites cried out for help, for someone to rescue them from slavery. God heard their cries. He sent Moses to win their freedom. Moses told Pharaoh, "The Lord God says, 'Let My people go.'"

But Pharaoh said no. Not once, not twice, but ten times he said no.

God sent horrible plagues—first turning all the water to blood and then covering the land with frogs. The frogs were everywhere—in houses, on beds, even in ovens. He sent flies and disease, hail and hungry locusts, darkness and death—until Pharaoh finally said yes. So the people prepared to go and the Lord led them out of Egypt.

What We Can Learn

The children of Israel are like all the children of God. We harden our hearts like Pharaoh (Exodus 7:13), but God uses things in the world—for the Israelites, it was blood, flies, and frogs, and worse—to save us. Just as He eventually used death to save the Israelites, He used death to save us. Jesus' death on the cross saved us from the eternal death that sin brings. Even better than the Promised Land God gave the Israelites, we will live forever in God's never-ending kingdom.

Hopping Frogs

In God's second plague on Egypt, He covered everything with frogs. Let's make some sugar "frogs" hop around.

What You Need

Metal bowl or coffee can
Plastic wrap
Rubber band
Sugar
Shallow metal saucepan
Metal spoon

What You Do

- *Cover a metal mixing or serving bowl with plastic wrap, secure it with a rubber band, and pull it taut. Or, take the lid off of a coffee can, stretch the wrap over the top of the can, and secure it with the rubber band.*

- *Put the bowl or coffee can on a flat surface, right side up, and sprinkle sugar on the plastic wrap.*

- *Hold the saucepan by the handle sideways (so it is perpendicular to the flat surface) about an inch away from the bowl. Bang on the pan with the metal spoon as hard as you can. What happens to the sugar?*

What's Happening

When you hit the pot, it vibrates, causing vibrations in nearby air molecules. The vibrations pass through other air molecules in waves that we call sound waves, which makes the plastic wrap vibrate and the sugar jump.

Crossing the Sea to Safety

Exodus 14–15

Moses and the Israelites left Egypt, but they weren't safe for long. Pharaoh changed his mind, and off his army went after them.

The Israelites saw them coming—chariot wheels churning, horse hoofs pounding—and they were afraid for their lives. Ahead of them was the Red Sea, a great body of water, and there was no way to the other side. But God held back the waters of the sea, and they walked across on dry ground.

Pharaoh's army thundered after them, and God let the sea come crashing down on them.

What We Can Learn

The outcome of this confrontation looked bleak, yet impossibly, Moses led the Israelites through the water to safety. God can accomplish the impossible. The Israelites were saved, but the enemy was washed away. Our Lord and Savior, Jesus Christ, does the same thing. With His Word and through Baptism, He washes away our sins and by offering forgiveness and grace, He saves us.

Floating Water

God held back the waters of the Red Sea so the Israelites could cross over to safety. We can make water stay in a cup, even when it's upside down!

What You Need

- Cardstock
- Scissors
- Clear drinking glass
- Water

What You Do

- Cut a square of cardstock so it's larger than the diameter of the glass. (A cereal box or the cardstock packaged with a photo frame work well.)
- Fill the cup to the brim with water and cap it with the cardboard.
- Press down on the cardboard (it will get wet) and quickly turn the cup upside down.
- Take your hand away. What happens to the water?

What's Happening

The water presses down on the cardstock, but air under the cup pushes up on the cardstock. The air pressure is greater than the water pressure, so the water remains in the cup.

The Fall of Jericho

Joshua 6

Can you make a tower of blocks fall without touching a single block?

To get to their new land, the Israelites had to fight their way through. The walled city of Jericho was in the way.

God told their new leader, Joshua, exactly what to do.

What a strange plan it was! They marched around the city for six days. Some priests carried the ark of the covenant and other priests blew rams horns. On the seventh day, they marched around Jericho seven times. This time the priests blew their trumpets, and all the people gave a mighty shout.

The walls of the city gave way! Jericho was theirs and Joshua gave the glory to God.

What We Can Learn

This dramatic story clearly illustrates our powerlessness. Joshua and the Israelites couldn't take Jericho on their own might. Only God could win the city for them. Just as the children of Israel knew that God was with them in the ark of the covenant we also know that God is with us, especially when we face challenges. On our own, we have no chance of knocking down the walls of sin that separate us from God. Only our Lord Jesus Christ can break through the barrier of sin.

Collapsing Walls

Joshua brought down the walls of Jericho without a fight. Let's make a soda bottle collapse without using a muscle.

What You Need

Soda bottle
Hot water

What You Do

- Fill the soda bottle half full with hot water and leave it uncapped.
- Swirl the water around for 30 seconds.
- Dump the water out and quickly cap the bottle. What happens to the bottle?

What's Happening

The hot water heats up the air inside the bottle. When the bottle is emptied and capped, the air begins to cool. Cool air takes up less space than warm air, so the sides of the bottle collapse from the force of outside air pressure.

Gideon Wins in Battle

Balloon Kazoos

Loud noises helped Gideon and his small army win their battle. Let's make a racket of our own using just balloons.

What You Need

Balloons

What You Do

- *Hold the balloon with one thumb and forefinger of one hand and with the thumb and forefinger of your other hand, pull the balloon neck out and back several times to stretch it. Then, blow up the balloon.*

- *Grasp the balloon's neck with the thumb and forefinger of both hands about half-way between the inflated part and the tip, and squeeze it so the air doesn't escape.*

- *Loosen the grip of your fingers on the neck by varying degrees, and sometimes pull your fingers apart, stretching the balloon neck out. What happens?*

What's Happening

What crazy sounds! The air molecules in the balloon rub against the molecules of the rubber balloon as they are released. The sounds change as the exiting air causes the neck to vibrate at different speeds.

Judges 7

Gideon was a faithful man of God. He lived in Canaan, the Israelites' new home. But, because of their sin, the Israelites were handed over to their enemy by God.

One day, as Gideon threshed wheat for food, the Angel of the Lord came to him. "The Lord is with you," the angel said. "Go and save Israel from Midian."

Taking only three hundred men, Gideon defeated the great enemy of God. At night, he gave everyone trumpets and jars. Inside the jars, he put torches of fire. The men blew their trumpets and shouted. They smashed their jars and waved their torches.

The enemy was frightened, and Gideon won—all without raising a sword.

What We Can Learn

Children might think of Gideon as a superhero. However, God chose Gideon, an ordinary man, to do an extraordinary job. And just as He promised, He helped him do it. Each of us has been chosen by God. Because Jesus keeps His promises, we know that He is always with us and will provide all we need. Remind your children of God's commitment to them. Because of what God has done for us, we can do the things He has planned for us.

Samuel Hears God

1 Samuel 3

Samuel was just a child when God called him. He was sleeping one night in the temple of the Lord when God said: "Samuel! Samuel!"

Samuel thought it was the priest Eli calling him, for he lived at the temple with him. He ran to Eli's room.

"What do you want?" he asked Eli. But Eli had not called him.

Three times the Lord God called Samuel. The fourth time, Samuel said, "Your servant is listening."

God wanted Samuel to give a message to Eli. From that day on, Samuel was known as a prophet, a person who spoke the words of the Lord.

What We Can Learn

God speaks and acts through many things of the world so we might know His mighty and gracious deeds. He also speaks through His Word, the Bible. God speaks to us through the writings of the Old Testament prophets, Jesus' words in the Gospels, and through the New Testament apostles. He works through these words to bring the for-giveness of sins Christ earned for us on the cross. The Bible gives us words God wants us to hear. That's why we should read it, memorize it, and share what we learn with others.

Ringing Bells

Samuel heard God's voice as clear as a bell. We can hear bells too, using just a spoon and string.

What You Need

Metal spoons
String

What You Do

- *In the middle of a length of lightweight string two feet or longer, tie a knot around the handle of a spoon.*

- *Wrap the string ends around each of your index fingers.*

- *Put your fingers in your ears, as though to block out noise.*

- *Swing the string against the edge of a piece of furniture, such as a table, so the spoon taps against it. What do you hear?*

What's Happening

The waves of vibrations we experience as sound travel better through a solid object than through air. When you tap the spoon against the table, the sound waves travel though the string and into your ears. You hear bells!

A Whirlwind Takes Elijah

2 Kings 2:1-18

Elijah was a faithful man of God. God chose Elijah to be a prophet—to teach people about God and His promises. In his life, Elijah did many miracles, deeds that showed he had God's power. He caused food to appear, fire to come from heaven, and life to return to a child.

He was walking one day with Elisha, his friend, who was also chosen by God to be a prophet. Suddenly, a fiery chariot drawn by fiery horses thundered between the two friends. A mighty whirlwind blew around them and it swept Elijah up into heaven. Elisha saw him go, and he wept when he saw Elijah no more.

Water Whirlwind

God took Elijah up to heaven in a whirlwind. Let's see what a whirlwind—or a tornado—looks like.

What You Need

2 soda bottles
Water
Electrical tape

What You Do

- *Fill one bottle about two-thirds full with water.*

- *Place the other bottle on top of the first, upside down, with necks together. Tape securely.*

- *Hold the bottles at a slant, like a forward slash (/), one hand on the bottom of the lower filled bottle and one hand holding the necks. Swirl the bottles rapidly in a circular pattern, using greater force with the hand holding the lower bottle.*

- *Stop swirling and flip the bottles over so the empty bottle is on the table. What happens to the water?*

What's Happening

For water to move in a circle, forces called centripetal ("center-seeking") forces must act on the water. Here, these forces are a combination of air pressure, water pressure, and gravity. As the water circles, friction between water molecules and the wall of the bottle causes water to pile up along the edge, drawing water from the center and allowing the water to drain in a spiral.

What We Can Learn

Elijah and Elisha were God's appointed prophets. In God's own time, Elijah was taken into heaven without experiencing death. We too will escape the finality of death with the assurance of eternal life through God's grace. Through His work, Jesus has overcome death for us: "Death is swallowed up in victory" (1 Corinthians 15:54).

A Woman's Oil Flows

2 Kings 4:1-7

Do you know how to help people who are poor? God wants us to help people in need.

Elisha, a man of God, knew a poor woman, a woman who had no money for food.

"What do you have?" he asked.

All she had was a little oil in a jar. Elisha told her to find more jars. She and her sons did what he said.

They poured oil from their own jar into jars they borrowed from friends. They poured and poured and poured. They poured until all the jars were full. When they were done, the woman sold the jars, and she had money to buy food for her family again.

What We Can Learn

In His mercy, God provided for the widow and her sons. When we pray, "give us this day our daily bread," we know the Lord will provide all we need, both for our bodies and our souls. God is active in our daily life through the things and people He provides. God's grace flows abundantly through His Word and the Sacraments. And He sustains us daily with His forgiveness through the work of Christ in our lives.

What You Need

2 small jars
Spoon
Water
White vinegar
Dish detergent
Baking soda
Glass baking dish

Overflowing Jar

Through Elisha, God filled to the brim all the jars the woman and her sons could find. Let's make our own jar overflow.

What You Do

- *Add 1/4 cup water, 1/4 cup vinegar, and 1/8 cup dish detergent to one jar and stir to mix.*

- *Put 1/8 cup baking soda in the other jar and set the jar into the baking dish.*

- *Pour the liquids into the baking soda. What happens?*

What's Happening

Vinegar is an acid and baking soda is a base (or alkali). They combine to produce carbon dioxide gas. The dish detergent adds foam to the chemical reaction.

David the Shepherd

1 Samuel 16:1–13; 17:34–37

It came time for God to choose a new king to rule the people of Israel. He sent Samuel, the nation's priest and judge, to the town of Bethlehem to the house of Jesse, a family that had eight sons. Samuel met each one, the oldest to the youngest.

The youngest, David, was a shepherd, a boy who was strong and able. When wild animals attacked his herd, he could snatch the sheep from their mouths.

When Samuel saw David, God said: "Anoint this one. David is your new king." And the Lord came upon David in power.

What We Can Learn

David provides us with the model of a shepherd: one who guides, guards, and provides for his flock. He was a humble boy, yet he was chosen for great deeds. David—a man after God's own heart (Acts 13:22)—pointed the way to Jesus. Jesus called Himself our Good Shepherd. The Bible says we are like sheep who have gone astray (1 Peter 2:25). Jesus, the Shepherd of our souls, brings us back.

Attack-Proof Water

The shepherd boy David protected his sheep from attacks by bears and lions. Let's see how we can "protect" water and keep it from spilling after an attack.

What You Need

- Plastic sandwich bag
- Water
- Sharpened pencil

What You Do

- *Fill the bag with water and close it with the zipper lock or a twist tie.*

- *As quickly as you can, stab the pencil into the bag and out the other side. What happens to the water?*

What's Happening

The bag is made from polyethylene, a type of plastic that shrinks when it is punctured. The plastic itself seals the holes the pencil makes as it enters and exits the bag. Despite the attack, the water stays put.

The Shepherd Who Sings

1 Samuel 16:14–23

After God anointed David, he went to serve King Saul. Saul had been a great king, but now he suffered very much. Saul did not listen to the Lord and now he was tomented. Saul's servants wanted to help him.

They called for David to come, for not only was he brave and strong, he played beautiful music on the harp. "The Lord is with him," they said.

So David lived in Saul's palace from then on. Whenever Saul was troubled, David would play soothing music for him.

Music is a gift from God to us. Songs are praise we give back to God.

What We Can Learn

In the psalms, we have a wealth of songs and prayers on a remarkably wide range of topics. The psalms are most beloved, though, because they teach us so clearly and eloquently that Christ died and rose for us. In this story, the Spirit of the Lord used David's gift of music to drive out the evil spirit that tormented Saul. Through David's music, the Lord soothed Saul and preserved David in Saul's household. God used David to bring to the world His plan of salvation in Jesus Christ—through David's family Jesus was born.

Comb Music

David was not only a fighter, but a music-maker who played the harp. We can create a simple instrument and make music ourselves.

What You Need

Pocket comb
Scissors
Tissue paper or waxed paper

What You Do

- *Cut a piece of tissue or waxed paper big enough to fold over the comb.*
- *Put the comb lightly against your mouth, with your lips slightly open.*
- *Hum a song. How do you sound?*

What's Happening

The paper vibrates when sound waves from your humming hit it. The vibration of the paper molecules turns your humming into a kazoo-like sound.

David Fights a Giant

Swirling Marble

To battle Goliath, David whirled his stone in a sling. Instead of slinging rocks around your house, let's contain our swirling "stone" in a bottle.

What You Need

Soda bottle
Marble

What You Do

- Drop the marble into the soda bottle.
- Tip the bottle upside down. What happens to the marble?
- Put the marble back into the bottle and, holding the bottle upside down, swirl it around in front of you. What happens to the marble this time?

What's Happening

Thanks to Isaac Newton, we know that an object will move in a straight line at constant speed unless acted upon by an external force. When the bottle is turned upside down, gravity pulls the marble down and out. When you swirl the bottle, friction and the walls of the bottle provide an external centripetal ("center-seeking") force, keeping the marble going around in a circular motion.

1 Samuel 17

Goliath was a giant—more than nine feet tall! He wanted to fight God's people, and everyone was afraid of him.

Young David said to King Saul: "As a shepherd, the Lord delivered me from wild animals while I watched my father's sheep. The Lord will deliver me from Goliath."

Goliath and his men laughed, but God was with faithful David.

Sneering, Goliath charged at him.

David put a stone in his slingshot, and—zing! He hit Goliath in the forehead. The giant crashed down onto the ground. Now everyone knew that the true God was with them.

David was a warrior, a shepherd, a music-maker. When he grew up, he became a great king. From his family, the Savior of the world would one day come.

What We Can Learn

Young, inexperienced, and vulnerable, David was an unlikely hero. Yet with God's help he saved Israel from a wicked giant who would otherwise have destroyed them. From David's line, another unlikely hero would come. God's own Son, Jesus, born in lowly circumstances to a family of no great wealth or renown, came to earth to save us from the wicked giant of our sins. Without Him, our sins would destroy us. With Him, our sins are defeated once and for all.

Safe from the Flames

Daniel 3

The Israelites once again became the slaves in the land of Babylon. Nebuchadnezzar, the king, ordered everyone to worship his gods.

Three faithful friends—Shadrach, Meshach and Abednego—refused to worship anyone but the Most High God alone. The king warned them they would be punished by being burned up in a furnace.

"Our God will protect us and deliver us," they said.

The king was furious and ordered the furnace to be made seven times hotter than usual. The king threw them into the furnace blazing with fire. But when he looked in, he saw them unharmed and walking around. With them, he saw a fourth figure, a divine messenger sent to protect them and to make God's power known.

When Nebuchadnezzar saw that God had protected the three friends, he became a believer in the one true God too.

What We Can Learn

The Bible tells many stories of miraculous rescue. This story shows how God rescues believers and saves them. The Messiah, the Son of God, protected these believers from the fiery furnace. In the same way, Christ suffered, died, and rose again to rescue us from our sins. The Messiah still rescues us through His Word and the "fire" of the Holy Spirit in Baptism.

Floating Marbles

God kept the three friends safe from the hot fire. Let's see how we can keep marbles safe from the cold water.

What You Need

Marbles
Water
Small plastic container

What You Do

- *Fill a sink with water.*

- *Drop three marbles into the water. What happens?*

- *Reach in and retrieve the marbles.*

- *Put your container into the water so it is floating and drop in the three marbles. What happens to them?*

What's Happening

This is an experiment in buoyancy. An object in water pushes down and the water pushes back up. The water can't push back hard enough to keep the marbles alone afloat because of their greater density. But the force pressing up from the water displaced by the container is greater than the weight of the container and marbles, so it floats. (You've just learned Archimedes' Principle!) How many marbles will your "boat" hold? Once the density of the container with its cargo exceeds the density of the water, it will sink.

d Shuts the Lions' Mouths

Daniel 6

The roar of lions is loud and scary, isn't it? Daniel once spent a night trapped with lions.

Daniel was a faithful man of God who worked for the king. Other rulers wanted to take Daniel's place. They knew Daniel prayed only to God. So they asked the king to make a rule that anyone who did not pray to the king alone would be thrown to the hungry lions.

The king did not want to hurt his friend, but because of the rule he had to lower Daniel into the lions' den. The next day, the king ran to the den and called, "Daniel, did your God keep you safe?"

Daniel shouted back, "My God sent His angel to shut the lions' mouths."

And the king believed in the living God just like Daniel did.

What We Can Learn

A man of God, Daniel was despised by those around him. A plot to destroy him resulted in his being cast to hungry lions, a certain death sentence. But Daniel trusted God and was delivered from the jaws of death, and others came to faith because of it. God sent an angel to rescue Daniel. In the same way, God sent Jesus to rescue us. Like Daniel, Jesus was also despised and a plot to destroy Him resulted in a death sentence. Jesus, who was God in the flesh, paid for our sins on the cross and defeated death. Through Him, we too are rescued from death.

Pepper Lions

Let's put pepper "lions" in a den and see how God keeps them away from Daniel.

What You Do

- *Fill the container with water.*
- *Sprinkle pepper over the surface of the water.*
- *Put a dab of dish detergent on your fingertip.*
- *Dip your fingertip in the water. What happens?*

What's Happening

Water is cohesive, meaning its molecules cling to one another and create a surface tension. The molecules of the soap break the cohesion of the surface, causing the pepper to shoot outward.

What You Need

Water
Small container
Ground pepper
Dish detergent

A Great Fish Saves Jonah

Jonah 1–3

God wanted the people of a great city, Nineveh, to hear of His love. God told Jonah to go and tell them. But Jonah ran the other way.

Jonah got on a ship and thought he was safe. But God sent a fierce storm.

He told the frightened sailors to throw him overboard because he was to blame for the storm. The storm stopped at once, and God provided a great fish to swallow Jonah whole. Inside the belly of the fish Jonah prayed to God. Jonah was inside the fish for three days, and then the fish spit him onto the shore.

Now, Jonah knew he should obey God. He brought God's message to Ninevah, and the people turned away from their wickedness.

What We Can Learn

Three days and nights in the cold, dark, airless belly of a fish. Three days in a cold, dark, airless grave. By sending Jonah, God showed His love and mercy to the people of Nineveh. By sending Jesus, God showed His love and mercy to all the people of all the world. God saved the people of Ninevah through the preaching of His Word. By reading His Word today, we can understand God's message of forgiveness through faith in Christ. When we live by faith in what Jesus accomplished for us, we have God's gift of salvation.

What You Need

- Clear bowl
- Hot water
- Uncooked egg
- Food coloring

Egg Whales

God sent a fish to swallow Jonah and keep him safe underwater. We can see Jonah breathing in an egg "whale."

What You Do

- *Put the whole, uncracked egg into the bowl, and cover it with hot water.*
- *Put a few drops of food coloring into the water.*
- *Watch closely from the top of the bowl. Can you see Jonah breathing inside the "whale"?*

What's Happening

Eggshells have pores. Through them, the hot water heats the air inside the shell, causing it to expand. The heated air escapes through the porous shell and forms lines of bubbles in the water.

Being with God

Bubble-in-a-Bubble

The song writer says he would gladly become a servant just so he could spend time in God's house. We can put ourselves in God's house by blowing one bubble inside another bubble.

What You Need

Bubble-blowing liquid or dish detergent

Water

Glycerin

Bubble wand

Straws

What You Do

- *If you have bubble-blowing liquid, use it to make your bubbles. To make your own, mix 6 parts water to 1 part dish detergent and 1 part glycerin (found in the skin care section of a pharmacy). For longer-lasting bubbles, let the mixture sit awhile.*
- *Using a bubble wand, blow slowly enough to make a large bubble. Catch the bubble with the wand and turn it upside down so the wand is on top.*
- *Wet the end of a straw with bubble liquid and shake off the excess.*
- *Poke the straw into the bubble on the bubble wand.*
- *Blow a bubble through the straw and shake your double bubble off the wand. What happens to your bubble?*

What's Happening

You can insert the straw in the bubble because a bubble is like a stretchy skin surrounding a volume of air. The bubble you blow inside won't last long, though. Because bubbles always seek a shape having the least surface area, bubbles that are close together will merge to share a common wall.

Psalm 84

Can you think of anything better than having everything you want? Every toy you want to play with, every yummy treat you want to eat, every friend you want to play with?

But long ago, a song writer said that being in the house of the living Lord is better than anything else: "A single day spent in God's house is better than a thousand days anywhere else." In his song, a Psalm in the Bible, he said he'd rather be a servant in God's house rather than have everything he wanted but live among people who don't love God.

More than anything else, believers should want to be in God's presence to receive His mercy and grace.

What We Can Learn

Psalm 84 opens with "How lovely is Your dwelling place, O Lord of hosts!" The writer of this psalm longs for God's house; no other place on earth compares. God's house—the church—is where the Lord meets with us today as a body of believers. It is there that we receive His gifts of faith, forgiveness, mercy, and salvation through His Word and Sacraments.

Part 2:

New Testament Stories

Jesus Is Born

Luke 2:1–20 and Matthew 2

In the dark night sky, angels shone brighter than the moon and stars. They led shepherds to Bethlehem, to a stable where animals lived. Inside, they found a newborn baby, snuggling close to His mother, Mary.

After a time, in the starry night sky one star shone brighter than the rest. It led Wise Men from far away to a special place. When they arrived, they bowed down and worshiped Jesus. They gave gifts to honor the child. They knew He was the Son of God.

Jesus was born on earth as a gift of God's love. All who believe in Him as Savior receive the forgiveness from sin He earned on the cross. All believers will live with Him forever in heaven.

What We Can Learn

Jesus, God the Son, came to earth as a baby. God led the Wise Men to Jesus by providing them, first, with Old Testament prophecy and then with the star to follow. God leads us to Jesus by providing us with His Word, the Bible, leading us to His miraculous means of salvation, and then giving us people to follow—pastors, teachers, and parents—who show us how to lead a life pleasing to Christ.

Floating Star

A star high in the sky lead the Wise Men to Jesus. Let's see if we can make a ball float in the air like a star in the sky.

What You Need

Blow dryer
**Ping-Pong®
or other
lightweight ball,
or an inflated
balloon**

What You Do

- *Plug in and turn on the blow dryer. Face the barrel upward.*

- *Place the ball or balloon in the air stream a few inches above the dryer. What happens?*

What's Happening

Air moving at high speed has lower pressure than air that is still. The air moving around the ball creates a pocket of low-pressure air. The ball balances in the pocket of low-pressure air, while the upward force from the air stream keeps it aloft. The scientific term for this phenomenon is Bernoulli's Principle. (If you don't have a blow dryer, try blowing steadily upward through a straw—it takes a lot of breath!)

Jesus at the Temple

Color Ring

In Jerusalem, Jesus was surrounded by teachers in the temple. Let's use water to make rings of color around Jesus.

What You Need

- Coffee filters
- Washable (water soluble) markers
- Spoon
- Water

What You Do

- Flatten out the filter. Draw a circle in the center with one of the markers.

- Drop a spoonful of water into the center of the circle and watch. What happens?

- Try the same thing using markers of different colors.

What's Happening

If the marker is made up of two or more pigments, they will separate in reaction to the water. Those that are highly attracted to the filter will move more slowly than those with a weaker attraction, causing the pigments to separate. The process is called chromatography, and what you've made is called a chromatogram.

Luke 2:41–52

When Jesus was a boy, His family went to Jerusalem to celebrate Passover. This is a Jewish festival to remember the night God protected His children from death. When the Passover feast was over, His parents started for home. But Jesus was missing! They turned back in a panic.

For three long days they looked and looked for their son. Finally, they found Him in the temple, surrounded by teachers of the faith. Everyone was awed by how much the boy knew about God.

But His parents had been so worried. "Why did You do this?" His mother asked.

"I must be in My Father's house," Jesus said.

Even then, Jesus knew He was God's Son.

What We Can Learn

As a 12-year-old Jewish boy, Jesus would be preparing to take His place in the religious community. But as the Son of God, Jesus already knew His place in God's kingdom. This Bible story teaches that Jesus was obedient to His earthly parents while He prepared for the work that God the Father had sent Him to earth to do—to live a sinless life, yet die for the world's sins.

John Baptizes Jesus

Mark 1:1-11, Luke 3:21-22

On earth Jesus had a cousin. His name was John. He had a special job to do—God wanted him to prepare the way for Jesus.

One day, John was baptizing people in the Jordan River. He told them, "I baptize you for the forgiveness of your sins with water, but someone more powerful will come and baptize you with the Holy Spirit."

Then Jesus came to him to be baptized. Down He went into the water, and when He came up the heavens split open and the Holy Spirit in the form of a dove came down to rest on Him.

"This is My Son," God the Father said from heaven. "In Him I am well pleased."

What We Can Learn

An Old Testament prophet called John, a "voice of one crying in the wilderness, 'Prepare the way of the Lord'" (Luke 3:4). So when Jesus appeared, John identified Him as the Lamb of God and explained, "for this purpose I came baptizing with water, that He might be revealed to Israel" (John 1:31). At Jesus' Baptism, the Trinity was clearly present—in Jesus, in the Holy Spirit, taking the form of a dove, and in the voice of God. The same is true when we are baptized in the name of the Father, Son, and Holy Spirit. Through faith, our sins are washed away once and for all.

Swirling Color

When Jesus was baptized, the Holy Spirit came down to rest on Him in the form of a dove. Let's make swirls of color descend in a glass of water.

What You Need

- 2 clear drinking glasses
- Water
- Ice cubes
- Small measuring spoon
- Food coloring

What You Do

- *Fill one glass with cold water and ice cubes. Let it sit for 5 minutes to get very cold. Remove the ice cubes.*

- *Fill the other glass with hot water from the tap.*

- *Squeeze a small amount of food coloring onto the spoon and drop the color evenly into both glasses. What happens in each glass?*

What's Happening

Hot water is less dense than cold water, so hot water rises and then sinks as it cools, a process known as convection. In hot water, the food coloring swirls around with the water's motion and quickly mixes in. But in the cold water, the coloring initially drops to the bottom, although it eventually mixes in as the water warms.

Jesus Chooses Apostles

Luke 5:1–11

Simon Peter was a fisherman. One day he was fishing, but he couldn't catch any fish. Jesus told him to try again. He did and his nets filled up with so many fish they almost broke.

When Simon Peter saw this, he fell to his knees and said, "Go away from me, Lord, for I am a sinful man."

Jesus said, "Don't be afraid. From now on you will fish for people!"

Simon Peter left his boat and followed Jesus.

Jesus chose twelve men who were special friends called apostles. He chose them so He could teach them and send them out to preach the Word of God to the world.

Paper Followers

People followed Jesus because they were attracted to Him and to His teachings. Let's see how we can attract bits of paper to a balloon.

What You Need

Paper
Balloon
Wool clothing

What You Do

*   *Tear the paper into tiny bits and scatter them across a small area on a table or countertop.*

*   *Inflate and tie the balloon. Rub it vigorously against the wool.*

*   *Hold the balloon over the paper bits. What happens?*

What's Happening

The paper bits jump up and down and some stick to the balloon. A balloon, like all matter, is made up of atoms with charged and neutral particles (protons, electrons, and neutrons). It becomes negatively charged when it is rubbed against wool. The paper is initially neutral, but becomes positively charged when its negatively charged electrons move as far from the negatively charged balloon as possible. Because the paper's positively charged protons are now closest to the balloon, the paper is attracted to it.

What We Can Learn

Jesus' apostles were specially chosen to receive the Gospel, and then trained to spread that Gospel message throughout the world. Our Lord called them to serve the Church. God continues to call some men to serve the Church as pastors. Their calling is to administer the means of grace—God's Word and the Sacraments of Holy Baptism and the Lord's Supper. As God's chosen children though, we are all equipped and encouraged to share the Good News of His love and salvation with others.

Praying to God

Matthew 6:5-15

Jesus often talked to God alone in prayer. He didn't just pray to God in church. He prayed while He was alone walking on mountains and in gardens. He thanked God for food, and He prayed in front of others too.

Because Jesus died for our sins and forgives us, we can talk to God too. Jesus taught us how we can talk to God. We start with His name—"Our Father who art in heaven." God hears us. He knows our needs and concerns. We can tell Him anything. We can ask for forgiveness and for help when we face trouble. God hears our prayers in Jesus' name.

What We Can Learn

God called us to pray without ceasing. We are free to go to Him at all times and in all places because Jesus reconciled us to God and intercedes on our behalf. Our loving heavenly Father promises to listen and answer according to His will. Therefore, we pray to ask Him to bring us in line with His Word and His will for us. When Jesus' disciples asked about the proper way to pray, He gave them the model for prayer, which we call the Lord's Prayer. All forms of prayer—confession, adoration, thanksgiving, intercession—are based on this perfect model.

Bubbling Prayers

Jesus showed us how to pray to God. Let's let our "prayers" bubble up to God.

What You Need

- Drinking glass
- Club soda or seltzer
- Salt
- Spoon

What You Do

- *Pour some soda into a drinking glass.*
- *Put a tablespoon or more of salt into the soda. What happens?*

What's Happening

The carbon dioxide (the bubbles) in the soda is a gas dissolved in a liquid (water). When the salt dissolves in the water, the water can't hold as much dissolved gas, so it escapes as bubbles.

Jesus Feeds a Crowd

John 6:1–15

One time, Jesus spent all day teaching, surrounded by more than 5,000 people. As it came toward evening, the crowd had nothing to eat. Only one little boy had brought anything—he had just five loaves of bread and two small fish.

Jesus took the boy's humble food and gave thanks. He handed it out, and handed out more, and handed out even more! Can you believe it? The fish and the bread multiplied to feed all 5,000 people. Everyone had enough to eat, and still there were twelve baskets left over.

What We Can Learn

Jesus' miracle of feeding 5,000 people shows the great love and compassion our Lord has for us: "When Jesus landed and saw a large crowd, He had compassion on them" (Mark 6:34). First Jesus fed the people's souls by teaching them about the kingdom of God. Then He fed their bodies. Miracles like the feeding of the 5,000 take place regularly in His church today. He gives us our daily bread through the world He created. The bread from heaven—the body and blood of Jesus—multiplies in the Lord's Supper. This is how the kingdom of God is present among us.

Mounding Drops

Jesus fed more people than His friends thought He could—thousands of people with just one boy's lunch. Let's see how many drops of water can fit on a coin—it's a lot more than you think!

What You Need

Quarter
Water
Drinking glass
Eyedropper

What You Do

* Put the quarter on a flat surface.
* Fill the glass with water.
* Fill your dropper with water and then squeeze out drops onto the quarter until it is covered (about 12 drops).
* Keep squeezing drops onto the quarter. What happens?

What's Happening

You might think that the quarter could hold only enough drops to cover the quarter. But because water molecules are hydrophilic ("water-loving") and stick to one another, surface tension allows you to mound up twice as many drops.

Jesus Stops a Storm

Matthew 8:23-27

Once, after a long and busy day, Jesus and His disciples got into a boat and set out across a lake. Jesus went right to sleep.

Suddenly, a raging storm blew in. It whipped up towering waves that rocked the boat back and forth. Jesus' disciples were afraid, and they woke Jesus. "Lord, save us! We are going to drown!" they cried.

Jesus asked, "Why are you afraid, you with such little faith?" He got up, ordered the wind and the waves to stop, and the storm stopped at once.

His disciples couldn't believe their eyes. "Who is this that even the wind and the waves obey Him!"

What We Can Learn

The disciples were in danger from the storm on the Sea of Galilee. Jesus demonstrated that He can save us. As God in the flesh, He held power over the world because He created it. With a word, He stilled the storm and the disciples' lives were spared. Our lives are rocked by storms caused by sin. Because of His great love for us, He can and does save us from those storms by saving us from sin, death, and the power of the devil.

Raging Seas

Nature obeys God, her Creator. Jesus ordered a storm to stop and it did. Let's create a stormy sea in a bottle.

What You Need

Large spice bottle or small water bottle, empty
Water
Blue food coloring
Baby oil or mineral oil
Child's toy (optional)

What You Do

- *Fill the bottle about three-fourths of the way with water. (A long, narrow bottle with a wide lid works well.)*

- *Add a few drops of blue food coloring. Put the lid on and shake the bottle to mix.*

- *Fill the bottle the rest of the way with baby oil.*

- *If desired, put a small water-themed toy (a boat or a fish, for example) in the bottle.*

- *Holding the bottle on its side, tilt it slowly up and down. What do you see?*

What's Happening

Water and oil are immiscible; that is, they don't mix. They remain separated even when you tilt the bottle, creating the effect of waves.

Walking on Water

Cornstarch Sea

Jesus could walk on water because He created nature and has command over it. Let's create a cornstarch "sea" and see what happens when you "walk" over it.

What You Do

- Put 1/2 cup of cornstarch in the container.
- Measure out 1/4 cup water.
- Gradually add the water to the cornstarch and stir until the mixture is fluid but hard to mix and cracks form but quickly fill in.
- Walk your fingers over the mixture. What happens?
- Walk your fingers over the mixture again. Midway, pause and let your fingers remain on the surface. What happens then?

What's Happening

This mixture (called a colloid) acts like a solid when you apply a force—walking your fingers across the surface—but like a liquid when your finger rests on the surface. Force causes the long molecules of the cornstarch to move closer together, trapping the water. Without pressure, the water molecules can move between the cornstarch molecules. (For more fun, roll the mixture into a ball. Then let it rest on your hand—ooze!) **Note:** *Dispose of the mixture in a trash can rather than the sink to avoid clogging your drain.*

What You Need

Water
Cornstarch
A small container
Measuring cups
A spoon

Matthew 14:22–36

Jesus once showed that He is God's Son by walking on water.

One evening, while praying on a hillside, He saw His disciples at sea, struggling against a mighty wind and towering waves. He went out to help them—walking on the water!

They thought He was a ghost and they were afraid. But Jesus said, "Don't be afraid. It's Me."

Peter said, "If it's You, then tell me to come to You." So Jesus said, "Come."

Peter got out of the boat and began to walk. But Peter became afraid and started to sink. "Lord, save me!" he cried. Jesus caught him, and they climbed safely into the boat.

The other disciples were amazed and said, "You really are the Son of God."

What We Can Learn

To people in Bible times, the wind and waters were mysterious and frightening. Old Testament writers often pictured God mastering the wind and water—driving and blowing them, walking, sitting, and riding upon them, and rescuing His people from them (Exodus 14:21–22; 15:8–11; Psalm 18:6–19; 29; 77:14–19). Storms can be especially frightening to children, but we can assure them that God is in control, and He can use creation to teach us and comfort us. We find true hope in His Word, even when we find ourselves in the midst of stormy situations.

Money from a Fish

Matthew 17:24–27

Rulers wanted Jesus and His apostles to pay money to keep the temple in good repair. Peter went to ask Jesus about it.

Jesus already knew what Peter wanted. Jesus told him, "Throw a fishing line into the lake."

Peter did as he was told. He caught a fish and pried open its mouth. From inside the mouth of the fish, Peter pulled out a coin. It was just enough to pay what he and Jesus owed.

How do you think the coin got there?

What We Can Learn

This Bible story depicts a wonderful lesson for us as baptized, redeemed children of God. When the temple tax was due, Jesus miraculously provided the tax on Peter's behalf. Jesus pays our debt as well. Although we are sinful and cannot keep God's commands, we do not pay the price for our sin, which is eternal death. We are exempt from damnation because Jesus gave Himself on the cross on our behalf.

Coin Drop

Jesus put a coin into the mouth of a fish. Let's try to keep a coin from dropping into the mouth of this "fish."

What You Need

Drinking glass
Water (optional)
3 x 5 card
A coin

What You Do

- *Fill the glass halfway with water. (The water is just for the sound effect so it is optional.)*

- *Place the 3 x 5 card over the mouth of the glass and put the coin on top of it.*

- *On the short side of the card, use your thumb and forefinger to flick the card off the glass. What happens to the coin?*

What's Happening

Did you think the coin would fly off with the card? This is a demonstration of inertia—Newton's First Law of Motion says that a body at rest remains at rest unless acted on by a force. Your finger is the force that moves the card, but because it does not act on the coin, it remains in place and drops into the glass.

Jesus Loves Children

Mark 10:13-16

One day, some parents brought their children to Jesus, wanting Jesus to bless them. His disciples tried to keep the children away. "Jesus is busy," they said. "Don't bother Him."

But Jesus brought the children near. "Let the little children come to Me," He said. He took them into His arms and placed His hands on them in blessing and said, "The kingdom of heaven belongs to them. Whoever does not have the same simple faith will not enter it."

What We Can Learn

Our Lord wants people of all ages to be forgiven and welcomed into His presence. Therefore, we bring even the youngest children forward to be baptized and receive God's gifts of faith and salvation. Jesus said, "Whoever does not receive the kingdom of God like a little child shall never enter it" (Mark 10:15). Regardless of age or education, we are helpless to achieve heaven on our own. We cannot believe on our own. We cannot trust on our own. The faith the Holy Spirit provides is a gift we receive. Like young children, we are to be receptive and open to the gifts of faith, forgiveness and the kingdom of God.

Hole-y Straw

Jesus loved children, but His disciples wanted to keep them away. Let's see how we can keep a straw from bringing your drink to you.

What You Need
Drinking glass
Something to drink
A straw
Straight pin

What You Do

- *Fill the glass with your drink. Put in a straw and take a sip. Easy!*

- *Take the straw out of your drink and poke 20 or more holes in it with the pin.*

- *Try again to drink from your glass. Easy?*

What's Happening

A straw works because sucking on it lowers the air pressure inside of it. The air outside the straw then presses down on the liquid and pushes it up the straw. But when air enters the punctured straw through the tiny holes, it keeps you from lowering the air pressure inside.

A Man Walks Again

Mark 2:1-12

Once there was a man who could not walk. He had four good friends. They brought him to see Jesus. But Jesus was in a house so crowded with people they could not get near Him. They took their friend on his mat up to the top of the house, made a hole in the roof, and lowered him down to Jesus.

Jesus saw the faith of these friends. "Your sins are forgiven," He said to the man. "Get up, take up your mat and go home."

And right away, he did! The man leaped up and walked home. And everyone praised God.

What We Can Learn

In this Bible story, Jesus showed the key to understanding the kingdom of heaven—forgiveness of sin. Because He is God, He forgave the man's sins, which was his greatest need. Only God can forgive sins. Then He healed the man's legs, again showing His power as God, the Creator. In our lives, we are crippled by sin. Through Jesus' work, we are forgiven of our sin and are no longer crippled.

Leaping Oil

Friends of a paralyzed man let him down through the roof to be healed by Jesus, and he leaped up and walked. Let's sprinkle salt "men" down through a "roof" and see them leap for joy.

What You Need

Tall drinking glass or clear jar
Water
Food coloring (optional)
Cooking oil
Salt

What You Do

- *Fill the glass with about 3 inches of water. If desired, mix in a few drops of food coloring.*

- *Pour in about 1 inch of oil (vegetable or corn oil; olive oil doesn't work well).*

- *Sprinkle salt over the glass. What happens?*

What's Happening

The oil floats on top of the water because it is less dense and because the liquids are immiscible (they do not mix). Salt, however, is heavier than water. When you sprinkle the salt into the oil, the grains sink to the bottom of the glass, carrying blobs of oil with them. As the salt dissolves in the water, the oil is released and floats back up to the top.

A Woman's Offering

Mark 12:41–44

One day, Jesus was in the temple watching as people put money into a collection box for the temple treasury.

Some rich people came, dressed in fancy, fine clothes, and they dropped in many coins—clinkety-clank, clinkety-clinkety-clank.

Then a poor woman came in, dressed simply and humbly, and she dropped in just two pennies—chink, chink.

Jesus knew that was the only money she had. "This woman has given more than the others," He said, "because she has given all she has."

What We Can Learn

All that we have—our health, our families, our possessions—comes from the hand of God. It is the daily bread we ask for in the Lord's Prayer. Because we are forgiven in Christ, we are God's children and He provides all we need. Everything we have belongs to Him. When we live our lives in faith and do what He calls us to do, it is worshiping by giving back to God. When we obey our parents, do our homework, and love our neighbor, we are giving back to God.

Bulging Water

A woman gave her only two pennies to the temple.
Let's see how many pennies we can drop into a full glass of water.

What You Need

Drinking glass
Water
Pile of pennies

What You Do

- *Fill the glass to the brim with water.*

- *Carefully begin to drop the pennies into the water. What happens?*

What's Happening

The surface tension of the water allows it to stretch and mound at the top to accommodate the coins. See how many pennies you can add before the water's "skin" breaks and spills out. It's a lot more than you think!

Jesus Gives a Girl Life

Luke 8:40-56

A father came to Jesus, sad and afraid for his twelve-year-old little girl. She was sick. While he was waiting to talk with Jesus, a messenger told him that his daughter had died.

Jesus said to him, "Believe in Me. Don't be afraid. She will be well."

When they returned to his house, the cries of many people met them. Jesus told the crowd, "She is not dead; she is sleeping."

Jesus gently took her small hand in His, and in a voice everyone could hear He said, "Get up, little one." At once, life returned to her, and she stood up.

Imagine how happy her parents were!

What We Can Learn

This Bible story is one of several in which Jesus restores life to someone who has died. Children may be afraid of death, but through this story and others they can know that because He is God, Jesus has power over death. Neither death, nor sin, nor the devil can defeat Him. And like this little girl, those who believe in Jesus as their Savior are raised to eternal life through Him. Romans 6:3-4 tells us that we are baptized into Christ's death, and because we are, we also are brought back to live new lives in Him.

Rising Girl

Jesus had the power to give a little girl life again. Let's make a "girl" lie down and rise up again.

What You Need

Small balloon
Marble
Drinking glass
Water
Soda bottle

What You Do

- *Blow a small puff of air into the balloon, enough to fill it but not enough to make it stretch.*
- *Pinch the balloon above the opening to prevent the air from escaping and stretch the opening around the marble as a seal.*
- *Fill the glass with water and drop in the balloon. It should float upright, so only the tip of the balloon is above water. Squeeze the balloon gently to remove air if it is too high above the water, or add air if the balloon sinks.*
- *Fill the soda bottle with water.*
- *Drop in the balloon and screw on the bottle cap.*
- *Squeeze the sides of the bottle and then release it. What happens to the balloon?*

What's Happening

When you squeeze the bottle, putting pressure on the balloon, the air bubble inside it becomes smaller and displaces less water. That reduces its buoyancy and the marble's weight pulls the balloon to the bottom. When you release the bottle, the air bubble in the balloon gets bigger and its greater buoyancy pushes it up again.

A Sheep Is Lost

Luke 15:1–7

Jesus told this story: A shepherd had one hundred sheep. One day, he counted them—one, two, three, four . . . When he got to the end, he had just ninety-nine sheep. One was missing.

The shepherd left the ninety-nine sheep and went to look for the one lost sheep. He was afraid it would be hurt or would not find its way home again. He finally found the sheep and carried it home, and he celebrated with his friends.

In the same way, heaven rejoices when just one person repents of his sin.

What We Can Learn

Jesus called Himself the Good Shepherd. When we sin, we stray from Him. Jesus continues to seek His lost sheep. To repent means to recognize our sin and turn back from it. When we repent, God and His angels rejoice that we have returned. In Word and Sacrament, God sends His Holy Spirit to help us repent. That's why we go to church—to hear His Word and to receive His gifts and to offer worship back to Him.

Escaping Lamb

Jesus said a caring shepherd would look everywhere to find just one lost little lamb. We can make one marble "lamb" escape from a line of marbles.

What You Need

Marbles
Vinyl placemat

What You Do

- *Set up four marbles in a line on a placemat on a flat surface, each marble touching the next. (The placemat helps keep the marbles in line.)*

- *At the beginning of the line, place a fifth marble a little bit apart from the line.*

- *With your finger, lightly flick that marble so it gently hits the first marble in the line. What happens?*

What's Happening

Flicking the first marble sets up a chain reaction: one by one, the marbles pass the energy they got from being tapped to the next marble. Because the last marble has nothing solid to pass its energy on to, it rolls away. How many marbles can you line up and still create the reaction?

The Greedy Son

Luke 15:11–32

Jesus told this story: A young man left his home, taking his share of his family's money with him. He spent it all quickly, and in no time he was poor and hungry. Even food fed to the pigs looked good to him! Alone and sad, he went back home. "I have sinned against heaven and you. I'm not good enough to be your son," he told his father.

His father greeted his son with great joy and gave him clothes and food to celebrate his return. But his brother was angry.

"How can you welcome him back after all he has done?" he asked.

"Your brother was lost to us," his father said, "but now he is found." And the celebration began.

What We Can Learn

This parable is a comforting picture of the kingdom of God, a picture of repentance and absolution. The message of this story is that the son recognizes his sin and repents. When he returns home, he is forgiven and welcomed with joy. Our Lord always calls us to repentance and absolution. He welcomes us back with the open arms of a loving father. As this parable shows, God's grace and mercy are showered on all believers.

Rocket Launch

The greedy son took off like a rocket once he got his money. Let's launch a rocket of our own.

What You Need

- Alka-Seltzer® tablet
- Water
- Film canister

What You Do

- *Fill the film canister about 1/4 full of water.*

- *Drop in half of an Alka-Seltzer® tablet and quickly snap on the cap.*

- *Put the canister upside down on a counter or tabletop and back up a few yards—don't hesitate! What happens?*

What's Happening

Mixing the water and Alka Seltzer®, which contains sodium bicarbonate and citric acid, builds gas pressure in the canister until it is blown apart from the lid. **Note:** *If you don't want a mess in your classroom or kitchen, do this activity outside.*

Ten Lepers Are Healed

Jumping Raisins

Jesus made ten sick men well. Imagine how happy they were! Let's make ten raisin "men" jump for joy.

What You Need

Club soda, seltzer, or clear soda

Pint jar

Raisins

What You Do

- *Fill the jar with the soda. (Use a new, unopened bottle or can. Open and pour it over the sink to contain any spewing.)*

- *Drop ten raisins into the jar, one at a time. What do they do?*

What's Happening

The bubbles in soda are carbon dioxide gas. Although the raisins sink, the gas bubbles attach themselves to the raisins and raise them to the surface, where the bubbles burst and the raisins fall again. (If you watch from the top, you can see the bubbles bursting.) When enough new bubbles attach themselves, the raisins are raised to the surface again.

Luke 17:11–19

When you receive a gift, what do you say to the giver?

Walking into a village one day, Jesus saw a group of ten men. They were very sick with a terrible disease called leprosy. They were not allowed to be with other people and they were lonely.

"Have mercy on us, Jesus!" they cried.

Jesus told them to show themselves to their priests. The men did as they were told.

As they went their way, they saw that they were healed of their terrible disease! But only one of the ten men turned around and went back to thank Jesus. Jesus asked, "Where are the other nine?" To the healed man, He said, "Go, your faith has made you well."

What We Can Learn

Leprosy was a hideous and painful infectious disease. Those afflicted were banished from their homes and communities. The ten lepers that Jesus healed were so overjoyed at being freed of this disease that they rushed away from their painful exile. Only one returned thanks to his Healer, and he received Christ's precious gift of salvation as well as healing. Sin itself is an eternal, hideous, painful, and infectious disease. Only God can save us from this disease. In the daily washing and renewal of Baptism, we are cleansed from this disease. Let's give thanks to our Lord for His healing and mercy!

Zacchaeus Climbs a Tree

Luke 19:1-10

There once lived a man named Zacchaeus. He was a very rich man, but he took money that was not his.

Jesus came into his town one day, and people crowded around him.

Zacchaeus wanted to see Jesus, too. But he was not very tall and he could not see over the crowd. Zacchaeus climbed a tree so he could see.

Jesus looked up, right at him, and said: "Zacchaeus, I want to come to your house."

Right away, Zacchaeus climbed down. The people in the crowd were angry because Jesus was going to eat with a bad man.

Later, at his house, Zacchaeus promised Jesus he would pay back all the money he had taken. Jesus said, "Today salvation has come to this house."

What We Can Learn

Despite the crowds of people there that day, Jesus chose to come to only one person—Zacchaeus—a lonely, sinful man. Through Jesus' teaching, Zacchaeus recognized his sinful ways and repented of them. Zacchaeus climbed a tree to get close to Jesus. Jesus used another tree—the cross— to bring us forgiveness for our sin and salvation. Through Jesus, Zacchaeus was a new person. We believe and are made new in Christ, too, when we are baptized into His kingdom.

Celery Trees

Zacchaeus climbed a tree so he could see Jesus. We can make "Zacchaeus" climb a celery tree— just watch!

What You Need

Drinking glass
Water
Red food coloring
Celery stalk with leaves

What You Do

- *Fill the glass with water and squeeze in several drops of red food coloring.*

- *Break off a stalk of celery with leaves—the pale inside stalks work best—and cut a bit off the bottom. (You can also use Queen Anne's Lace, if it's blooming, or a white carnation.)*

- *Set the glass on a sunny window and watch it over a period of time. What do you see happening?*

What's Happening

The water travels up tiny tubes (called xylem) in the stalks and when it reaches the top some of it evaporates. Because water molecules stick together, more water is pulled up the tubes. Eventually, the leaves or flowers become the same color as the water.

Jesus Heals a Blind Man

Gooey Mud

Jesus used mud to give a man born blind his sight. Let's make a gooey mud to play with.

What You Need

- Water
- White glue
- Measuring cup
- Glass bowl
- Borax (powdered)
- Food coloring (optional)

What You Do

- Squeeze 1/4 cup of glue into a measuring cup and stir in 1/4 cup of water. Add food coloring, if desired. (You can use colored school glue instead. Some food colorings incorporate into the mixture, while some rub off.)
- In the bowl, mix 1/2 tsp. Borax with 1 tbsp. hot water. Let cool. (You'll find Borax in the laundry detergent aisle.)
- Pour the glue solution into the Borax solution.
- Stir the mixture—with your hands if you dare!—until you have a thick blob. (If any liquid remains, you can prepare another Borax solution and combine it with the remaining glue solution.)
- Take the blob out of the bowl and knead it with your hands until it firms up. How can you play with it?

What's Happening

White glue is made up of polymers that become suspended in water and slip and slide over one another. The Borax is a borate—a naturally occurring mineral—that causes the polymers to link together in a suspension. You've created a non-Newtonian fluid that becomes more solid with force (rolling it, tearing it, bouncing it) and more liquid at rest.

John 9:1–12

Jesus saw a beggar by the road. The man was blind—he had never seen anything in his life. The disciples asked Jesus if the man was blind because he sinned or because his parents sinned.

Jesus told them the man was blind so God's will could be shown in his life.

Jesus made some mud, mixing spit with the dust of the ground, and covered the man's eyes with it. Jesus told him to go to a pool of water to wash. The blind man did as he was told. After he washed himself, he could see!

He told everyone, "I was blind, but now I see!"

Some people did not believe him, but the man knew it was the truth.

What We Can Learn

In this story, a man's blindness is used to reveal God as the Creator and Savior of the world. Although we may have sight, we are all born blind and live in the darkness of sin. Jesus, the light of the world (John 8:12), banishes the darkness and brings us to God's grace. Sometimes it is God's will that we be strengthened through suffering, as this man was. God can use a hard situation to teach us that His will is always that we have faith in His healing and forgiveness. Like the blind man, we can know that our faith in Jesus Christ heals us from sin.

Jesus Dies and Rises

Matthew 27:11–28:10

Jesus fed and taught people. He protected and healed people. But most of all, He came to earth to suffer punishment for our sins and to provide forgiveness for the whole world.

God sent Jesus to die for us. He was accused, laughed at, beaten, and put on a cross to bear our sin. In a tomb, He lay dead for three days.

On the third day, early in the morning, caring women came to His grave. They were sad, for Jesus was dear to them.

An angel greeted them: "He is not here! He is alive!"

Jesus had promised that He would rise from the grave. And He did! Truly, He is the Son of God!

What We Can Learn

God the Son humbled Himself and came to earth to live a holy and perfect life, to bear the weight of all the sin of all the world for all time, and to die under that weight. God's glory is revealed on the cross. This is how He brings forgiveness and salvation to the world. God the Son comes to earth today in the means of grace—His Holy Word and the Sacraments of Baptism and the Lord's Supper. On our own, we cannot reach God. But He comes to us and gives us the gifts of forgiveness and eternal life with Him.

Swirling Mist

Two women came to Jesus' tomb early in the morning, only to find that He had risen from the dead. Let's make a swirling morning "mist."

What You Need

Shallow dish
**Cream
or half 'n' half**
Food coloring
Dish detergent
Spoon
Toothpick

What You Do

- *Pour the cream into the dish. Let it settle. (Milk will work, but cream adds zing.)*

- *Squeeze drops of a few different food colors into the cream.*

- *Squeeze a little dish detergent into a spoon. Dip a toothpick in it and then dip the toothpick into the middle of the dish of cream. Watch closely. What happens?*

What's Happening

The food coloring forms solid drops in the cream because the fat in the cream prevents the water-soluble coloring from mixing in. But dish detergent breaks up the fat and loosens the cohesive force between milk molecules, allowing the coloring to swirl around in it. You can keep the swirling motion going by dipping a detergent-coated toothpick into the solid streaks of color that form.

Fish for Breakfast

John 21:1–14

One day, after Jesus died on the cross and rose from the dead, seven of Jesus' disciples went fishing. They fished from a boat all night, but they caught nothing—not one single fish!

At dawn, a man called out from the shore: "Try again—on the other side of the boat." So they did. And did they ever catch fish! The net was so full they could hardly pull it in.

One of the fishermen saw the miracle and confessed his faith. "It is the Lord!" he said. Filled with excitement, Peter jumped from the boat and swam to shore.

The others rowed to shore with their catch, where Jesus was cooking breakfast over a fire. Together, they ate fish and bread. Now they knew that Jesus was alive.

Cork Fishing

After Jesus rose from the dead, He cooked His followers a breakfast of bread and fish that He provided. Let's see if we can catch a cork "fish."

What You Need

A bottle cork
Knife
Drinking glass
Water

What You Do

- *Cut a 1/4-inch slice of the cork, so you have a button-shaped piece of cork.*

- *Fill the glass to the brim with water.*

- *Try to float the cork in the middle of the glass. Can you do it?*

- *Remove the cork and gently add more water until the water surface bulges over the rim of the glass. Try centering the cork again. What happens?*

What's Happening

Before the water bulges over the top of the glass, you can't center the cork. It almost jumps to the side of the glass. But when the water bulges due to surface tension, it forms a convex surface and the cork floats on the highest point in the center.

What We Can Learn

In this Bible story, Jesus calls His apostles together and feeds them. He uses this time to prepare them for what is coming in the trials ahead. Jesus also restores Peter, who had betrayed Him, into a right relationship with Him again. Jesus keeps His promise to be with us to the end of the world (Matthew 28:20). He calls us together around a meal as well—the Holy Meal of His body and blood. In this Sacrament, Jesus restores us, and we remember His work that takes away our sin and makes us pure.

Jesus Returns to Heaven

Matthew 28 and Acts 1

A great many people saw Jesus alive after He had died on the cross—as many as 500 people at one time, and as few as one person alone.

Jesus told His disciples to go all over the world, teaching people about the kingdom of God and baptizing them in the name of the Father, the Son, and the Holy Spirit. "I am with you always, to the end of the world," He said.

One day, when He was with His disciples, Jesus was taken up into the sky. They all saw it happen. They could not take their eyes off Jesus. He disappeared into a cloud.

Suddenly, two angels were among them. "Jesus has gone to heaven," they said. "But He will surely return someday in the same way He went to heaven."

What We Can Learn

In the fulfillment of the Old Testament prophecy of Isaiah 7:14, Jesus is our Immanuel (Matthew 1:23), which means "God with us." Prior to His ascension, Jesus gave His apostles the Great Commission to preach the Gospel and baptize people in the name of the Father, the Son, and the Holy Spirit. Until His return on the Last Day, He promises to be with us always, "to the end of the age" (Matthew 28:20). He is with us—in His Word, in the Sacraments, and in our lives—so we are eyewitness of His grace, just as the disciples were eyewitnesses of Jesus' return to heaven.

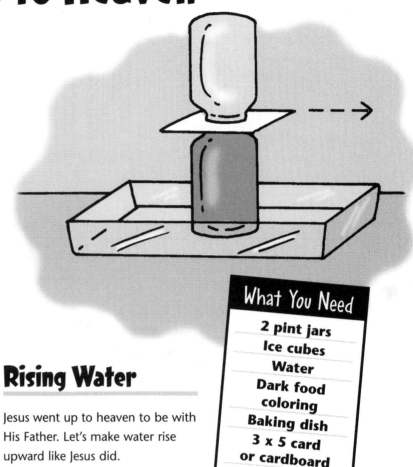

Rising Water

Jesus went up to heaven to be with His Father. Let's make water rise upward like Jesus did.

What You Need

2 pint jars
Ice cubes
Water
Dark food coloring
Baking dish
3 x 5 card or cardboard

What You Do

- *Fill one jar with cold water and drop in a few ice cubes to make the water very cold. After 5 minutes, remove the ice cubes.*

- *Fill the other jar with hot water. Put in a few drops of a dark food coloring. Place this jar into the baking dish.*

- *Put the index card over the top of the cold-water jar and quickly flip it over, holding onto the card as you do. Position that jar over the hot water jar, matching the mouths exactly to prevent spills (that's why you need the baking dish!).*

- *Hold the jars securely by the mouths and quickly slide the index card out. What happens to the colored water?*

What's Happening

Hot water is less dense than cold water, so the hot water rises. You know it's happening because you see the colored hot water swirling up into the top jar.

Philip Shares the Gospel

Acts 8:26–40

One day, Philip, one of the apostles, was walking along a road when along came a carriage. Inside, an important man from Ethiopia, a faraway land, was reading Isaiah's book in the Bible. He could not understand a word of it, so Philip got into the carriage and told him the Good News about Jesus.

Together they rode along and came to a place where there was water. The man from Ethiopia asked, "Why can't I be baptized?"

Philip baptized him, and then went on his way, preaching about Jesus.

What We Can Learn

Throughout His ministry on earth, Jesus forgave and healed, taught and preached. At His ascension, He gave this responsibility to His apostles, saying "Go therefore and make disciples of all nations, baptizing them in the name of the Father and of the Son and of the Holy Spirit" (Matthew 28:19). From that time until the End Times, Jesus will give this responsibility to called servants like Philip—pastors—who act in His place, teaching, preaching, and administering the Sacraments. The Lord calls each of us, too, young or old, to serve God in everything we do and tell others the Good News about forgiveness and salvation in Christ.

Reading Glasses

The Ethiopian man needed help from Philip to understand what he was reading in the Bible. Let's get some help reading by making a simple magnifying glass.

What You Need

- 3 x 5 card
- Scissors or hole punch
- Plastic wrap
- Tape
- Small images
- Eyedropper
- Water

What You Do

- *Cut or punch a small hole in the center of the 3 x 5 card.*

- *Tape a piece of plastic wrap over the hole.*

- *Place the card over a small image from a magazine, newspaper, website printout, or elsewhere. (An image you can barely make out with your eye enlarges the most dramatically.)*

- *Fill the eyedropper with water and squeeze out a big drop on top of the plastic-covered hole. Can you see the image now?*

What's Happening

A water drop is a simple plano-convex lens—one side is flat, one side curves out. Lenses like these, when used in telescopes and microscopes, enhance our vision by enlarging images.

List of Materials

You will not need all of these materials. Some activities can be set up with alternate materials that are listed here along with the primary materials.

Non-perishables

Baby food jars
Baby (mineral) oil
Baking dish
Balloons
Blow dryer
Borax (powdered)
Bottles (empty spice, water)
Bowls (clear)
Bowls (mixing, metal)
Bubble-blowing liquid
Bubble wand
Butter knife
Cardboard
Coffee can
Coffee filters
Coins
Comb
Cork
Crayons
Cups
Dish detergent
Drinking glasses (clear)
Eyedropper
Film canister
Funnel
Glue (white)
Hole punch
Knife
Marbles
Markers (water soluble)
Measuring cups

Measuring spoons
Paper (white, 8 1/2" x 11")
Pencil
Ping-Pong® balls
Pins (straight)
Pint jars (clear)
Pitcher (clear)
Placemat (vinyl)
Plastic sandwich bag
Plastic container (small)
Plastic wrap
Rubber bands
Ruler
Saucepan (shallow metal)
Scissors
Soda bottles (plastic)
Spoons (metal)
Straws
String
Tape (clear)
Tape (electrical)
Tape (masking)
Thread
Thread (embroidery)
3 x 5 cards
Tissue paper
Toothpick
Toy (small, water-themed)
Waxed paper
Wool clothing

Perishables

Alka Seltzer®
Baking soda
Bread
Carnation blooms (white)
Celery
Cereal (O-shaped)
Club soda
Cooking oil (vegetable or corn)
Cornstarch
Corn syrup
Crackers
Cream (heavy)
Eggs
Food coloring
Glycerin
Half 'n' half
Ice cubes
Milk
Pepper (ground)
Queen Anne's Lace blooms (white)
Raisins
Salt
Seltzer
Soda (clear)
Sugar
Vinegar (white)
Water
Yeast (rapid rise)

Selected Bibliography

Books

Breckenridge, Muriel, et al.
365 Super Science Experiments.
New York: Sterling Publishing
Co., 2001.

Finke, Stephanie.
Exploring Weather.
Uhrichsville, Ohio:
Promise Press, 2000.

Gold-Dworkin, Heidi.
Fun with Mixing and Chemistry.
New York: McGraw-Hill, 2000.

Marxhausen, Kim.
*It Only Takes a Spark:
40 Active Faith-Building Talks.*
St. Louis: Concordia Publishing
House, 1998.

Pearce, Q. L.
*60 Super Simple
Science Experiments.*
Los Angeles: Lowell House
Juvenile, 1998.

Pearce, Q. L.
*60 Super Simple More
Science Experiments.*
Los Angeles: Lowell House
Juvenile, 1999.

Pearce, Q. L.
*60 Super Simple Still
More Science Experiments.*
Los Angeles: Lowell House
Juvenile, 2000.

Websites

Chem4Kids (www.chem4kids.com).
Children's science education and activities.

The Exploratorium (www.exploratorium.edu).
Museum of science, art, and human perception
in San Francisco, California.

Fat Lion (www.fatlion.com).
Children's science experiments.

A. C. Gilbert's Discovery Village
(www.acgilbert.org).
Children's museum in Salem, Oregon.

Little Shop of Physics
(littleshop.physics.colostate.edu).
Science outreach program of Colorado State
University.

Reach Out! (www.reachoutmichigan.org).
Science mentoring program sponsored by the
University of Michigan.

Reeko's Mad Scientist Lab
(www.spartechsoftware.com/reeko).
Science experiments for all ages.

Science Made Simple
(www.sciencemadesimple.com).
Online magazine.

Scripture Index

Scripture Index